The Blue Bed
Natania Rosenfeld

SPUYTEN DUYVIL
New York City

© 2021 Natania Rosenfeld

ISBN 978-1-956005-04-2

Cover: "Floating" by Megan Williamson

Library of Congress Cataloging-in-Publication Data

Names: Rosenfeld, Natania, author.
Title: The blue bed / Natania Rosenfeld.
Description: New York City : Spuyten Duyvil, [2021] |
Identifiers: LCCN 2021036092 | ISBN 9781956005042 (paperback)
Subjects: LCGFT: Poetry.
Classification: LCC PR6118.O85 B58 2021 | DDC 823/.92--dc23
LC record available at https://lccn.loc.gov/2021036092

For

Ruth Danon

and

Gabriel Levin

Contents

I.

Journey to Berlin   11
Sacrificial   12
Adult Child   13
Mammography   14
In the Blue Bed   15
Beret   16
Father-Daughter Configurations   17
Spring in Berlin   19
Late Summer   20
Lake Efforts   21
The Green Shoes   22
The Journey   23
Aboriginal   24

II.

Lack   29
Memento   30
Autumn, Late Afternoon   31
Imbalance   32
Full-Length Portrait of a Dead Woman, Egypt   33
Degas' Bathers   34
Soutine, *Flowers and Fish*   35
Unquiet Landscapes: a series   37
I couldn't see   41
Watching *Amazing Grace* at the End of Passover   43

After Mendelssohn   45

Watching *The Elephant Man* Again after 36 Years   46

Arrival in London   48

III.

Fire   53

Nighttime   54

Nick   55

Graveyard   56

Return   58

Accommodations   59

Woman and Dog in Waning Light   60

Evening Idyll with Strange Fruit   62

Talisman   63

Country Company   64

House of Laurels   65

A Day in Central Park   67

Song, Birds   69

Falcon   70

Psalm   71

Evening   72

Making Love to Ben Webster   73

Notes   75

Acknowledgments   77

I.

I

Journey to Berlin

On the plane, reading Celan,
I heard you, Mother, your German
with the *r* that rolls closed.

When we thrust into strange
currents, I felt you in
the breathing all around.

In the reborn city streets,
I see you: fur coat, lipstick,
cigarette, laughing, exhaling

smoke, back then when artists
talked all night near the Wall.
Tired of palaver, never at home,

neither German nor Jew, credulous
nor eloquent, you flew back
to exile, silent husband, shy

child who held books all day
and came to you with questions
you've never answered.

SACRIFICIAL

The ram waits
to intervene. One
is always needed,
for somewhere—

everywhere—there
is a father with a knife
over his child. (Or a
mother, sharp-tongued,

quick to hit.) If only
every bush held a ram,
patiently entangled,
head bowed for the cut.

In the museum, I gaze
at one from Rome, mouth
in a firm line like
an old man's, resigned,

horn circling the labile,
downturned, tongue-
ear, facing the altar.
I quail, then think

Better you than me.

Adult Child

Much rests on
rain, light—
also the pores

open, shut.
Always, an old man
taught me,

finish your bath
with cold water.
Skin will close

into self.
You will know
your blood's

warmth
from others'
desires.

MAMMOGRAPHY
for Audrey Petty

After winter tending mother's flesh,
easing the bony torso to its finish,
you glimpse her shadow
in the oncology hallway.

You left the baby howling, banged
the car on your way here. Days,
weeks, you've lost keys, burned
pans, let water overflow.

The vise bears in as if
to squeeze out life. *No*, you say,
waving the shade back, *Not now.*

In the Blue Bed

I lay with my friend,
her head against mine,
her sadness in my ear.
Her pulse beat hard,
I said what I could.

I lay with my man.
Our bare bodies said
I attend. Our blood
whispered *Don't
depart from me.*

I lay sick and troubled,
blue quilt to my chin.
A violin moaned.
Life is a storm said
the bow to the strings.
We long and long,
we bruise
our throats and cut
fingers to coax
arias from wood.

On cobalt fields, at last
I dozed. Lie down, my
loves. Hold me, watch
the sails unfurling, fill.

Beret

Strange word for so simple
a thing as a flat, felt hat.

Don't forget your bear-ay,
my mother'd say, and I thought it

a protective object. Surely it wasn't
an "affectation"? Father despised

"affectation," and so did Mother: *She's
affected*, they'd say of one, and that

would be the end of *her*. Where were
the lines? Was Papa wholly un-"affected"?

Such questions were absorbing. Also,
Am I bad? Why the sudden slap?

And why, for a man without pretense,
a Parisian dauber's headgear? Why,

for the South Philadelphian, talisman,
not tallis? German, embraced and

cherished, not Yiddish. Swabian,
indeed, including a rustic embroidered

smock for me. But a *French* hat, with
the "t" unspoken. Why and why?

FATHER-DAUGHTER CONFIGURATIONS

Dream

I and Father, wearing trenchcoats, lost in railroad station. Father pulls in what I know to be the "wrong" direction: not to our intended train— or to it. I tug at him: "Papa, not that way, this way!" He's hard to budge, but moves with me when I lead. He extracts gloves from pockets and I help him fit them on his white, cold hands. My fingers grip his arm. Around us, panicked crowds. The air beneath the high ceiling is turgid and chill, steamy from trains and the breath of nervous, hurrying people.

Yesterday evening

I read about both Charlotte Salomon and Eva Hesse parting from their
    fathers at German railway stations.
Charlotte never saw Albert again, but Eva and her Papa were reunited in
    Amsterdam, where Albert died years later, broken by Sachsen-
    hausen and unspeakable loss.
Eva's father sometimes called her "Evchen," a diminutive that resonates.
I've known these "-chens" since I lived in Stuttgart at six, the age at
    which Eva fled Germany.
When my father writes, he sometimes calls me "Tokhtr." He'd be "Tateh"
    in Yiddish, but I call him Papa since our Stuttgart year. *Ah-ah*,
    the two sounds like an infant's gurgle; *P-p* like the lips' effort to
    blow bubbles.
When you elongate the *ahs*, they achieve effects of warmth and gravi-
    tas appropriate to a woman over fifty and a man of eighty-five,
    sitting together on a bench by a pond, watching finches, talking
    of the past as a heron wings over—

Also

need arising, shorter *ah*s can convey urgency
like gunfire, to seize attention among crowds
bent in layers of winter clothing, jostling,
rushing, stumbling to a platform.

Spring in Berlin

It rains and rains
I wear my black coat

on sidewalks I look down
for gold bricks

not gold, but bronze
but to my eyes golden

cobbles bearing names
of Jews who once lived here:

when they were deported
what camp they died in

usually Auschwitz
they are the relief

from the gray
how odd it is

that my light should come
from names of the dead

beneath my feet.

Late Summer

The windows are shut.
The soul, trying to escape,
is stuck: a suffocation, senseless.

Oh child, how could you?
Why didn't you wait?
When I reach the sill,

it is too late to release you.
You are always here
now, stale and cheated.

Lake Efforts

Last week a boy
lobbed stones. Each
time he threw, he turned

with a shout
but the grownups
weren't listening.

He chose bigger stones
and bigger, turning
every time. They

sat laughing, deep
in talk and drink.
What would it take

to disturb them—
a boulder? And how
would he find,

lift and heave,
a boulder? Audience
must be given, boy,

it can't be won. This,
at my age, in our age,

I know.

Green Shoes

Bought in defiance for turning
fifty-five, they look at me from

the ends of my legs, saying I'm
both old and a child. Buster

Browns: remember? Coming home
from the shoe store with mother,

Mother napping, Buster I called
the left, Brown I called the right.

They talked without motion. Is mother
all right? Is she angry? Let's go

on a voyage. No, she said to stay
here and admire you. No punish-

ment for clean soles on the window-
sill! Shall I lick them? Black soles,

smell of the shop, pomade of the man
who touched my feet, pressed hard

my big toe. I heft foot to nose, sniff,
put out tongue. Touch the tip—

one flick, doesn't count. (Does it?
Buster says no, Brown yes.) Tongue

back in mouth, shoe at ledge. I see
a cardinal in the branch.

O red friend, come inside!

The Journey
Luis Cruz Azaceta, 1988

Mine is a huge eye,
likewise my nose looms

Both bend toward
the hold of the boat

that is also I
and contains souls

who require my care
lying exhausted

unmoored intertwined

.

My face is caged,
lashed in a red mesh

a rage of inflamed veins
a rope-net of blood

White arrows impale
the back of my skull

my neck cannot unbend
trammeled as it is

and we are solitary
in a black striated sea

the boat and I,
the boat-I.

Aboriginal

I went to the ocean
the ocean was churning
with filth   I went to
the shore the shore
was carpeted in bones

I went to the mountain
there were corpses
on its peak   I went
to the lake and looked
down, down, down

at the bottom of the lake
was a fish   the fish was
God and blew bubbles
I made a long spear
from many arrows put

together   I impaled
God   I put God on
a fire made from
the broken arrows

As he roasted he spoke
Here is what you
must do he said,
After you eat me,
you must walk up

the mountain, you must
pluck down the skulls
you must go to the ocean
you must take a great net
and collect the filth,

you must spread it care-
fully and plant my bones
Then, he said, and here
is the hardest part, you
must go to the shore

you must sit down
and wait for the wave
when it comes you must
not budge   you must let
the tsunami take you away

If you do this, a new fish will come
but only if you sing my song
while the wave drags you under
and you are gasping for breath
and here is my song, said the fish,

I will tell it to you while you eat me.

II.

II.

LACK

A round table,
two places, each

with propped
book, a halved

egg on each plate,
paprika on each half:

Mother bear, Father
bear, where are you?

And where is my
plate, my spicy egg?

Memento

My friend paints
her father's hairbrush
again and again in ink

in gouache and oil
numinous now as
Fra Angelico's halos

and see: his curling
white hairs
almost speak.

Autumn, Late Afternoon

Wind has blown all day.
Amber branches roil
outside the panes.

My hand on pillow of
upper arm, fingers
touching silk-white head,

I nap beside Mother.
When dark fills
the window, we awaken.

IMBALANCE

F's got vertigo
M fell down
he crouched
to help her up
He got up and
fell down
He lay on the couch
and put ice on his head
She decamped
to her garden
A pink petal stuck
to her skirt

now it's on the floor

Full-Length Portrait of a Dead Woman, Egypt

Her right sandal
tests the threshold
but the left's
stepping sideways,
out of the frame.
Her round face
is a gold fruit—

We want her so,
we thrust her back
to the garden
where she fled.

Degas' Bathers

It needs washing,
this body:
in middle age,
our skins no
longer shine.

One climax
tires us, it is all
our flesh can take
to hold
the beloved inside

and let him
go again.

Soutine, *Flowers and Fish*

On the news in the "hottest
summer on record": even

fish are nervous, the ponds
and lakes too warm for

their thin scales. Pity them,
pity the old in Paris garrets,

choking on sun and dust,
where Soutine hungered

till the age of thirty.
In the lower left, the fork

assumes the animal's
sinous shape. Scarlet

flowers mock the gaping
mouth, the tail mimics

the base of a vase or
a wineglass. The fish

is streaked with blood,
background is night,

plucked flowers scream
as they thrust forth and spill.

The fork pities the fish
it prepares to pierce.

The painter with his brush
slathers his own wide eye,

his striated flesh, outrage.
Now, he would paint

the fish in flames
like huts in a burning village.

Unquiet Landscapes
for Jenny Hager

It is reasonable to conclude that the fact of having been raped was less significant to [her] sense of self than some . . . have suggested.
　　　—Rebecca Mead on Artemisia Gentileschi

I. Recluse

I have seen this before:
a woman bows
holding her child
before a charred field

What remains
of trees thrusts upward
knobbed, accusing

Late light points
the wrong way
I shall hide
beyond horizon's
yellow smear

II. The Things We Lost

Our favorite horse,
his eye welkin-
filled.

The house that once
was safe. Afternoons
of rapture.

And gained: sun
rolling to the end of sky
like billiard

into pocket.

III. Moralist

It is a luxury
to make pronouncements
from behind a screen of trees.

The sun's red yolk
will find you out.

IV. Manifold

Sea's rage washes
light pink beach,
bleeds like ink
from a Chinese letter,
sweeps and pools
toward our feet.

Red stripes declare
good sailing tomorrow.
What monarch rises,
crowned and purple,
into darkest night?

V. High Land

From here
I see so far
old wounds
are scribbles,
driftwood
on desert sand.

VI. An Infinite Grace

A ball, bowling
down the horizon,
sees its image
on the scored roof
of a barn.

Bleeding red bands
across the blue fields,
it keeps its form,
fends all assaults.

VII. Ebon

Lollipop,
haloed in disaster,
dancing.

We must aspire
toward our own
dark hearts.

I Couldn't See

but you showed
me: a blue ravishing
guarded by a burning

orange sphere.
I saw too
the rift, the two

Thebes: of the living
and the dead,
and the one

where the empress
bore seven children
by the sun's prophet.

Like the blind king
I saw but didn't see,
felt, but knew not.

Billows lifted me,
raw red silk,
flutes and drums

battered my ear.
The people
had skins of ochre

and walked with
wrists entwined.
All this you

have been showing me.
You made me feel
you knew me

before I knew myself.

Watching Amazing Grace at the End of Passover

Two nights
half a century ago
a woman

with the voice
of Miriam
hailed freedom

Last night, a woman
took bullets
for her rabbi

.

Today we sit
in a darkened cinema.
In camera's light,

sweat weds mirrored
spangles on Aretha's
chin, her throat

stretches, carries
shimmering cries
to rafters. Did she

holler like this, giving
birth at twelve? Or
when her man

struck? Did her screams
bring mercy, or rending
and more blows?

Mary, don't you weep.

The Reverend leaps
to mop her slick
brow, then flings

the soaked cloth
straight at camera's eye.
Sing it, Mary,
part the sea.

After Mendelssohn
Joan Landis, z"l

The spire gleams
on a late summer noon,
holding its face to the slate
face of sky.

By a hot grate, in black,
dust on his bare, black arms,
a man howls
without sound.
Legions
howl this way. And

from a stone mouth,
clear water tumbles.
Little dresses and dogs
on leashes rummage
in grass. Stylish

nymphs sashay
under enormous orchids,
wreathed in coffee auras.

And there *she* was. Ebony
tunic, amber beads, behind
the filigreed door.
Cellos went off.

The spire, blue like water,
dumb. Sun passing, bus
fumes, bird of paradise
at the corner where the red
man changes to green.

Watching *The Elephant Man* Again after 36 Years

Pistons, steam, child labor,
night streets, whores, drink,
dirt, fog, jostling crowds—

in the center of it all a white-
skinned man, shining, a
natural aristocrat of no

dropped aitches or lapses
in etiquette. Soulful eyes
glinting from bulbous

incoherent flesh, he stumbles
in the streets like Jesus at
the stations, his last words

"It's finished" (Lily Briscoe,
too), barely a hint of Hannibal
the Cannibal in his noble, pained

benefactor's hooded eyes,
or suggestion that Power
complies in poverty's sins,

no view of Barbados, Jamaica
or the men and women
whose faces gave no light

who received only lash and brand,
next to whom even John Merrick
the circus feature was "a man,

not an animal, a man," son
of an angelic mother, not
of any stampeding beast.

Porcelain, powder, ladies' gloves,
white, the very stars in the sky
welcome him as theirs at last

as he lies back in bleached
sheets and gazes upward.

Arrival in London

I wallow in the tub,
news in my wrinkled
hands, its shouts of murder,
disasters and movie stars.

Last year, a whale lost
her way, drifted up the Thames.
Now, I read, her skull's
displayed to crowds.

In the African music shop
below, exiles sway
to headphones. A tide
of traffic thrusts at the kerb.

I sink; water covers
me. Farther down, I hear
the Underground's thump,
Behemoth calling her mate.

The water drains, workers
in dark coats tumble down
the street like mollusks. Naked,
I stand at the window.
No one's looking.

III.

III.

Fire

Under circling swifts,
I ignored omens,
missed the turning, followed
an emerald dress, a black
boot. I lit the fire.

The house was burning,
small birds fell.
They were too young,
without tail feathers.
A bird mother can't
lift her infant.

What hand lit this? You
stood by, black-haired,
pale cheek throbbing.
Where were our
keepers? They did not
confer, or clasp in brotherhood.
Each guarded
his own lashed heart.

Firepeople came, with axes
and water. Steam rose from
the roof. Some children
looked on: at that age
disaster is amusing,
and even death is droll.

Nighttime

When did I acquire
this bulldog
hairy as a Scottish
heifer

or orangutan
endearing
but stubborn
I pull so hard
he pulls in the other
direction

his lower jaw
juts with
determination
I tug and pant

I have another dog
more pliable
Why don't I give up

and leave this one here?

Nick

1475-85; obscurely akin to Old English gehnycned *wrinkled,*
Old Norse hnykla *to wrinkle*

You nicked me
now give me back,
un-wrinkled.
In your pocket,
I became
a crone. Heart like
a sagging bag, you,
thief, like the doctor
who said I had
a hoary womb,
pierced it.

Senescent or not,
it still bled, a mystery
solved only with
a kind of arrow,
whose point
had me gasping

like Teresa with
her robes about her—
so many beautiful
folds! Each upon each
like layers of skin
one sloughs off
lifelong, flayed
by one's own
thieving
disposition.

Graveyard

She presses five new
plants above him

tramps to the well,
pewter cans hanging

like millstones from
roughened hands.

.

Arcs of silver bow down
the green stems. So many

death has called
to bloom and stay.

.

Remembering his gaze,
goatish and red,

my tongue cleaves
to my palate.

Quiet, indignant,
I observe her care.

.

It seems to me
she lies. Or

after loss,
truth twists.

Body is frail.
Soul, the same.

Consolation, a must.

Return

His hands like winter earth
greeted my landing.
He made a blue bed
above the old white room
where I used to weep.

A washing bird,
I rocked and stretched
in his arms.

At breakfast, his palm
opened: my time of arrival
penned on flesh,
a scrawl of stems.
He offered an egg,
pillow seeping light.

I toured the garden:
fig tree, lettuce,
flowers of squash, before
he left. Alone in
his home, I wandered
the rooms. At the end
of the hall, my body:
a willow in his mirror.

Accommodations

When there are frogs in the house,
install ponds, said a voice in my head

lying down in the reek of a summer
afternoon. All month the house has smelled

of shit and charred meat. Perhaps the workers
who left smears on our walls and footmarks

on floors dug up something below us
and whatever's there is festering. I'm lighting

incense against the stench, reading books as if
they could stanch the very horrors they record.

Frogs, come: I'm making room, pouring water.

Woman and Dog in Waning Light

Snow's fallen, we're off to the park. I slip
on the slick sidewalk, you trot with nose up,

glancing bright-eyed, inquiring, at my face.
I don't know, little one. Purblind, I'm with

you on the voyage. You dash when I release
you, return at my call: every day, this is a wonder.

.

All week, I've leafed in the book of Ice Age art,
your head in the crook of my arm. Here are

man-beasts, bison with thin legs, and women,
massive, boulder-thighed, sack-breasted,

clefts ineluctable as the first apple.

.

Without you, my Alabama hound, I'd
know nothing past my own nose tip,

might look up, not down; might hear
birdsong not whisperings underfoot,

not voice of leaves scent of leaves
twinkling of leaves flashing   smell

of leaf-mold   smell of others. I need
you to tune me to the world

of blood and pulse and exhalation,
mud and root, chaser and prey.

.

Three milennia ago (fathom that!) a child
and wolf found ingress to this cave: see, here,

the little foot marks, the paw pads in a circle.
Bloodred handprints shrilled when they came:

I was here! Farther in, sinuous antlers, flanks,
tusks like grass in wind. Undulant shining

menacing muscles flaring flexing   a presence
a protection (so the two must have felt).

Strangest yet, this bison's head above a woman's
mound. The child paused to clean her torch

and stayed some time. After her departure, rubble
filled the mouth again—until just recently, following

a sniff of air, three hominids crawled in. On a shimmering
screen, we see what they saw. Outcrops limbs and members

thrusting forward, dark grass in storm. Now,
walls everywhere flutter, massless. Even at the end,

they'll flicker. I'll hold you as long as I can.

Evening Idyll with Strange Fruit

In the sea-green park
the dog leaps in puddles,

coats his legs. Home,
he offers each paw

in turn to my soft cloth.
Now, in the red-and-verdant

living room, evening arrives,
Cassandra Wilson croons. From depths,

a phrase climbs her throat, hangs
in the window's breeze. Last week

over coffee, my friend told me
her Alabama great-uncle had been—

No one spoke of it. The story
would tear the tongue, rend

eardrums. It despoils my shelter.

Talisman

Little photo
I clutch in my palm:

elm that quells
my heat,
canopy that shrouds
my dream,

a nightmare
of history from which
I awakened bone sick.

One small face, a green
shirt, and eyes
like leaves.

Stalwart, sturdy.
Inheritor of no pain,
at most one drop of fear,

shining
in a yellow frame—

Country Company

I know exactly why I dreamed the dream. That we were in a place twenty miles from where we used to live, a bleak "city" on the plain. A place smaller and just as poor, but more real. The pale, bowed people were human beings who wanted beauty. I broke in somehow, needing direction, to a trailer. I found a family. I found small children who talked up a beautiful storm. Their mother offered me whatever I might want, though I saw she had little, and less of what I'm accustomed to. The boy was drawing a seven-branched candelabrum. I offered, in return, all that I could add. When the mother left the trailer, I began to wash her kitchen window, to clear the view of fields for her.

I worked hard at it, scrubbing at the whitened pane while the boy continued talking to me. I thought, *We are going to be comrades. We are going to make common cause.* I went out to softly fading daylit fields. The road I walked on was quiet, mine for the moment, the strip ahead bathed in purpling light, bent stubble all around, fierce dry grasses glowing. I saw all I'd previously failed to see. Had seen at moments, on occasion. Saw now, ineluctably. Returned to the boys and the mother who wanted me. I know why. It was a place I lived, unknowing and lonely. It was a book I read afterward. And voices I heard, telling buried stories.

House of Laurels

First the house itself
        then the house's subdivision:

a degree of squalor
        or at least, disorder,

rooms of different sizes
        cut off from one another,

with no hallway. I was supposed
        to come back here

and complete something, but
        which is my room

and who is the landlord? Is he
        the man I loved then?

Still here, or long gone? (I know
        that soon he'll die.)

Who are these other women?
        "The diligent ones,

with ribbons and pins." Was
        I not diligent? "Not

shining, not pat." But I remember!
        there was an attic, a little

cat, my supple shoes she chewed
        on the day of my test.

"You should have defended yourself
> better. You should have risen

above your gnawed shoes." I bought them
> especially, and a lavender dress

with fluted Grecian folds. Am I
> here to try again? "Yes, if

you can move into a room. But
> it seems all are taken."

May I speak to the landlord?
> He loved me once.

A Day in Central Park
for LJ

I.

You take oars, guide us
under hanging branches.
In the willow's

silence, our voices fall.
Clouds furl, woes
unravel, Sibelian

melodies.

II.

Near the dock
a pigeon flails
in brownish water.

I lift the ash-gray
flopping frame. She bites
my white hand-flesh,

drags her self away
fast as she can, a bruise
against the pavement.

We leave in drizzle.

III.

On stage, in turquoise silk
and sequined sandals
fighter's brow furrowed

your arm chastises
the violin. In the final
movement, thunder

peals out. You push on
carrying us
through turbulence

to shore.

Song, Birds
—for Stuart Cooke

The male lyre bird,
my friend tells
me—the Superb
from SE Australia
and Tasmania, and the
Albert's from Queensland—
creates a song to attract a female
that could almost be dubbed opera,
or is, in fact, opera, a one-man opera
with instrumentation. The Albert tugs
on vines and clacks their leaves together,
and those vines, attached to a canopy above,
make all the trees in the vicinity quiver, undulate
and shake while he, with his double larynx, keeps
a double tempo, percussive on one side, melodic on
the other, seduction by polymorphousness. The female,
however, is a seasoned critic. Listening with head cocked,
she produces a rating based on the history of lyre bird song,
accepts or rejects depending on originality of the opera in question.

The Superb, on the other hand, also a musician and composer, with a wider
range and a longer song cycle covering a more diverse swath of the
continent, using different accents, as it were, and possessing a tail
with far more feathers, a truly magnificent (superb) lyre of a tail,
that he throws over his head in a shimmering, glimmering
tent, says my friend, throwing his hirsute arms over his
bald head so that the brown hairs shimmer in the low
lighting of the café where we sit on cushions telling
stories—the Superb is a visual as well as an aural
artist, and constructs special mounds from leaf-
litter, dirt and mulch, like the brush turkey,
and stands on those mounds to rise above
the surrounding terrain, and makes music
fit to seduce a queen, if she adjudges
it fine enough and grants her favors.

FALCON

Talons claw at bark,
breast catches in branches'
crotch, heaves
at ebon trunk—

Thrumming: hard fruit
on a bush. Fire crackles,
clouds rush to make storm.
A moment, and the seams are rent.

Away from you, master.
Circling among my fellows.
Hunting whom I will.

Psalm

In the new year,
I awoke to a gardener's
soft shears. On my bed,
viburnum cast its form.
Some hush had made
fences greener,
insects crowd together,
singing final notes.

I felt your pulse
ticking in my arms.
Leaves stood still,
unstained. The last
cicadas crackled,
night capsized
in breaths of gray.

I heard you, you
tested me, like god
trying out a microphone.

Evening

You cross the floor, holding a peach.
On your foot is a green leather slipper of the sort called *babouche*.
You lift one leg balletically so as not to step on the dog
who is worn out from the walk we all just took
and the many things he wanted to greet or devour,
and you are smiling because you know I am in a delicate state,
and the green *babouche* is like a mango skin, or a forest,
and in the forest are swift foxes, suspended in the air for a moment,
through which my heart flies straight to the overstory
to rest between green branches.

Making Love to Ben Webster

Ben Webster pulls
the blankets away
bares the sheets

laves our flawed shapes
with yellow notes
draws us deep

gives the melody
and the beat a
sudden contrapuntal

swerve; swirls
around the bed
and lifts it up

knowing nothing
at all of two white
ageing bodies in Chicago

forty years after
his passing, making
love to him.

Notes

"Father-Daughter Configurations": Charlotte Salomon, German painter killed by the Nazis after emigrating to France. Eva Hesse (1936-1970), Jewish artist who fled Hamburg, Germany with her family as a small child to settle in New York and became arguably the most innovative American sculptor of the twentieth century..

"The Journey" is a painting by Cuban-American artist Luis Cruz Azaceta in the Allen Memorial Art Museum, Oberlin, Ohio.

"Soutine, Flowers and Fish": Chaim Soutine, Lithuanian-French Jewish painter, 1893-1943.

The poems of "Unquiet Landscapes" are inspired by, and titled after, works by Los Angeles-based abstract painter Jenny Hager.

"I Couldn't See" was inspired by Jenny Hager as well, but also by the Metropolitan Opera's production of Philip Glass's *Akhnaten*.

"Country Company" is for Sarah Smarsh, on reading her book *Heartland: A Memoir of Working Hard and Being Broke in the Richest Country on Earth*

"Watching *Amazing Grace* at the End of Passover": the singer was Aretha Franklin, recorded at the New Bethel Baptist Church in Watts, Los Angeles, 1972.

"Making Love to Ben Webster": Ben Webster (1909-1973), "King of the Tenors," was a jazz saxophonist.

Acknowledgments

The following poems first appeared in these journals:

"Beret" and "Nick," *The Yale Review*, Winter 2019. ("Beret" received special mention in the Puschcart Prize Anthology, Fall 2020.)

"Mammography," *Calyx*, Fall 2014.

"Arrival in London," *Cave Wall*, Fall 2010.

"Spring in Berlin" and "Sacrificial," *Gettysburg Review*, Fall 2014; Spring 2018.

"Recluse," "The Things We Lost," and "Moralist," appeared alongside images of the Jenny Hager paintings that inspired them, *Yew* journal November 2013.

Gratitude

Embedded through this book are the presences of those who have held and inspired me: above all, always, Neil Blackadder. My beloved parents, Stella Pagales Rosenfeld and Sidney Rosenfeld. My friends Audrey Petty, Jenny Hager, Jaspreet Singh, Leila Josefowicz, Lynette Lombard, Tony Gant and Michael Amin Hamilton. And, of course, Ruth Danon and Gabriel Levin.

I am thankful also, for thoughts and support from Kitty Bancroft, Monica Berlin, Brandi George (through Black Lawrence Press), Zali Gurevitch, and Arne Weingart.

And to the patient, caring, mysterious and clever TT and Aurelia at Spuyten Duyvil: I couldn't have asked for more!

And to Ross White, convener of The Grind, for helping me to produce daily work and giving me a forum in which to share early and late drafts of many of these poems.

And finally, to Knox College, for supporting the time and travels that gave space for poems to arise.

NATANIA ROSENFELD is a writer, independent scholar and Professor Emerita of English at Knox College. This is her second book of poetry, after *Wild Domestic* (Sheep Meadow Press 2015). She has published a critical book, *Outsiders Together: Virginia and Leonard Woolf* as well as an e-chapbook, *She and I* (Essay Press). Her essays, poems and fiction have appeared in journals including *AGNI, The Yale Review, APR, Raritan, Gettysburg Review, Michigan Quarterly Review,* and *Southwest Review*, and four essays have been listed as "Notable" in *Best American Essays* collections. She was recently named one of 30 "Writers to Watch" by the Guild Literary Complex in Chicago, where she has lived since 2018.

www.ingramcontent.com/pod-product-compliance
Lightning Source LLC
Chambersburg PA
CBHW011406070526
44577CB00003B/400